Karl Marx **Friedrich Engels**

Manifesto of the Communist Party

(Also known as *The Communist Manifesto*)

Translation from German by
Daniel Deleanu

LogoStar Press

Toronto

ISBN: 978-1-105-49072-9

Printed and bound in the USA.

(1) A frightening spirit is stalking throughout Europe – the spirit of communism. All the powers of Old Europe have joined in a holy exorcism of this spirit – the Pope and the Tsar [the Russian Emperor], Metternich [famous Austrian statesman who had to resign because of the 1848 Revolution, in the year when this *Manifesto* was published] and Guizot [French Prime Minister between 1847 and 1848], French Radicals [Alexandre Auguste Ledru-Rollin, etc.], and German police officers.

(2) Where is the opposition party that has not been accused of communism by its adversaries in power? Where is the opposition party that has not hurled back the scarring reproach of communism back at the head of the more progressive opposition members, as well as at those of its reactionary opponents?

(3) Two things surface from considering these facts.

(4) Firstly, communism is already recognized as a power by the ruling powers of Europe.

(5) Secondly, it is high time that the communists present before the world their points of view, their goals, their tendencies, and oppose the fairy-tales about the frightening spirit of communism by a manifesto of the Party itself.

(6) In order to achieve this goal, communists of different nationalities have gathered in London and produced the following manifesto, which will be published in English, French, German, Italian, Flemish, and Danish.

I

Bourgeois and Proletarians

(7) The history of all society has thus far been the history of class struggles.

(8) Free people and slaves, patricians and plebeians, nobles and serfs, guildsmen and journeymen – in short, the oppressors and the oppressed, stood in unvarying opposition to each other carrying on a continuous struggle, sometimes open, sometimes hidden, a struggle that always ended either in a revolutionary alteration of the entire society or in the common ruin of the hostile classes.

(9) In the earlier epochs of history, we find almost everywhere a sophisticated division of society into various ranks, a variety of grades in social status. In ancient Rome, we find patricians, knights, plebeians, and slaves. In the Middle Ages, we have feudal lords, vassals, guildsburghers, journeymen, and serfs. In addition, each of these classes had further subdivisions.

(10) Modern bourgeois society, which emerged from the ruins of feudal society, has not abolished the antagonism of classes. On the contrary, it has only substituted new classes, new conditions of oppression, and new forms of struggle for the old ones.

(11) Our epoch, the epoch of the bourgeoisie, is distinguished, however, by the fact that it has reduced the antagonism of classes to its simplest form. Society as a whole more and more tends to be divided into two great

classes directly confronting each other, namely the bourgeoisie and the proletariat.

(12) From the serfs of the Middle Ages emerged the burghers of the first towns; from these municipal communes sprang the primal elements of the bourgeoisie.

(13) The discovery of America and the circumnavigation of Africa established new grounds of action for the rising bourgeoisie. The East Indian and Chinese markets, the colonization of America, the colonial trade, the increase of commodities generally and of the means of exchange, all these gave an impulse, until then unknown, to commerce, navigation, and industry, and this caused a rapid development of the revolutionary element in the decaying feudal society.

(14) The old feudal system of industry, under which production was no longer the interest of guilds and monopolies, was not sufficient anymore for the growing demands of the new markets. Therefore, the feudal system was replaced by the manufacturing one, and the guildsmasters were pushed out by the middle-class industrialists. Thus, the division of labour in one and the same workshop followed the division of labour between the different corporations of guilds.

(15) Nevertheless, since the markets kept constantly growing, the demands always increased. At this point, steam power and machineries revolutionized industrial production. Then, manufacture was replaced by modern large-scale industry; the industrial middle class was replaced by the industrial millionaires, and the chiefs of entire industrial armies by the modern bourgeois.

(16) Large-scale industry has established the global market, for which the discovery of America smoothed the way. The global market has boosted enormously commerce, navigation, and land communication. This boost, in turn, has positively impacted the expansion of industry; and in the same proportion as industry, it has reacted on the expansion of commerce, navigation, and railways, in the same proportion the bourgeoisie developed, increased its capital, and pushed into the back all the classes descended from the Middle Ages.

(17) We see, therefore, how the modern bourgeoisie is itself the result of a long process of development of a series of transformations in the modes of production and exchange.

(18) Each step in the expansion of the bourgeoisie was accompanied by a corresponding degree of political progress. An oppressed social estate under the rule of the feudal nobles, armed and self-regulating association in the commune, here independent urban republic, there taxable third estate of the monarchy, then, during the period of the manufacturing system, a counterpoise against the nobility in the semi-feudal monarchy based on estates or in the absolute one, and a cornerstone of the great monarchies generally, the bourgeoisie has, at last, since the establishment of large-scale industry and the global market, gained for itself exclusive possession of political power in modern representative states. Modern governments are nothing else but committees for the management of common affairs of the entire bourgeois class.

(19) The bourgeoisie has played an extremely revolutionary role in history.

(20) The bourgeoisie has obliterated all feudal patriarchal, idyllic relations wherever it has managed to come to power. It has callously destroyed the various feudal ties that bound people to their "natural superiors," and has left no bond of union between human beings other than the sheer self-interest of cash flow. It has drowned the holiest paroxysms of religious fervour, of chivalrous enthusiasm, and of pious feelings in the ice-cold waters of selfish calculation. It has transformed personal dignity into market value, and in place of the numerous non-forfeitable chartered freedoms, it has established a single freedom, which is totally devoid of conscious – the Free Trade. In a word, the bourgeoisie has replaced the exploitation concealed under religious and political illusions with the open, shameless, direct, blunt exploitation.

(21) The bourgeois stripped the halo from all professions considered until then sacrosanct. They have converted the medic, the lawyer, the priest, the poet, and the scientist into their paid servants.

(22) The bourgeoisie has torn the touching veil of sentiment from the family tie, having it reduced to a mere monetary issue.

(23) The bourgeoisie has shown how the brutal display of vigour in the Middle Ages, which reactionaries so much admire, has found its befitting complement in the most indolent lassitude. It has been the first to reveal what people can achieve through their active force. It has performed wonders that exceed the Egyptian pyramids, Roman aqueducts, and Gothic cathedrals. It has carried out expeditions that far surpass all human migrations and crusades.

(24) The bourgeoisie cannot exist without constantly revolutionizing the instruments of production, hence the relations of production – that is, all relations of society. Persistence in the old modes of production was, in contrast, the first condition of existence for all the preceding industrial classes. A constant modernization of the modes of production, uninterrupted upsetting of all social conditions, and endless insecurity and restlessness distinguish the Bourgeois Epoch from all earlier ones. All olden ties existent among people, with their procession of primeval august conceptions and prejudiced beliefs are becoming extinct, and the new ones grow old before they can become firmly rooted. All that is fixed and stable peters out, all that is holy is desecrated, and people are ultimately coerced to face with a sober vision their position in life and their reciprocal relations.

(25) The need for an ever-expanding market for its produce drives the bourgeoisie over the entire globe. It must create new settlements, nuzzle everywhere, and make connections in all those places.

(26) Through the exploitation of the global market, the bourgeoisie has given a cosmopolitan tendency to the production and consumption of all countries. To the great regret of the reactionaries, it has deprived the industrial system of its national ground. The time-honoured national industries are now being destroyed on a daily basis, in case they have not been destroyed already. They are being superseded by new industries, whose implementation is turning into a vital question for all civilized nations, whose raw materials are not indigenous, but imported from the most distant of lands, industries whose products are

consumed not only domestically, but also globally. In place of the old desires, quenched by domestic products, we find new ones, whose gratification requires the produce of the remotest zones and climates. In place of the old regional and national self-sufficiency and isolation, we find a universal interaction, a multilateral interdependence of nations. This happens not only in the material world, but also in the intellectual one. The intellectual creations of individual nations become universal property. National one-sidedness and mental limitation become less and less tolerable, and out of the many national and regional literatures a universal literature is now taking shape.

(27) Through the quick improvement of all means of communication and the incessantly facilitated communication, the bourgeoisie draws all nations, even the most barbaric, into civilization. The cheap prices of its commodities are its heavy artillery with which it levels down all Chinese walls to the ground and makes even the toughest xenophobia surrender. It forces all nations, under penalty of annihilation, to adopt the bourgeoisie's mode of production; it forces them to implement its so-called civilization in their lands – that is, to become bourgeois. To put it in a nutshell, it fashions a world after its own image.

(28) The bourgeoisie has subjected the rural community to the ruling tenets of the city. It has created immense urban areas. It has greatly increased the size of the urban population as compared with the rural, and thus has rescued an important part of the population from the idiocy of rural life. Just as it has made the countryside dependent on the city, so it has made the barbaric and semi-

barbaric countries dependent on the civilized ones, the peasants on the bourgeois, and the East on the West.

(29) The bourgeoisie thins out more and more the diffusion of the population, of the means of production, and of ownership. It has agglomerated the population, centralized the means of production, and concentrated property in a few hands. The necessary consequence of this was political centralization. Independent provinces and those loosely confederated, with different interests, laws, governments, and taxation systems were merged into one nation, one government, one juridical code, one national class interest, and one customs frontier.

(30) The bourgeoisie, during its class rule of about only a hundred years, has created more massive and more gigantic forces of production than all preceding generations put together. The subjection of the forces of nature to humans, machineries, the application of chemistry to industry, agriculture, steam navigation, railways, the electric telegraph, the clearing and cultivation of entire continents, the canalization of rivers, large populations conjured up out of the ground – what earlier century could have imagined that such forces of production slumbered in the haven of social labour?

(31) We have seen that the means of production and exchange on whose basis the bourgeoisie was built up were produced in feudal society. At a certain stage in the development of these means of production and exchange, the conditions under which feudal society generated and transformed the feudal organization of agriculture and manufacture, in short, the feudal relations of property no longer matched the already developed productive forces.

They hindered production instead of developing it. They turned into so many fetters which had to be broken – and they were broken, indeed!

(32) They were superseded by free competition along with the social and political constitution suited to it, along with the economic and political rule of the bourgeois class.

(33) A similar movement is going on before our eyes. The bourgeois relations of production, exchange, and property, a modern society that has conjured up such huge means of production and exchange – this is even as the sorcerer who is no longer able to control the powers of the chtonian world he has evoked. For decades, the history of industry and commerce has been nothing else but the history of the revolt of modern forces of production against the property relations that are the conditions of existence for the bourgeoisie and its rule. It is enough to mention the commercial crises which, by their periodic recurrence, question the existence of the entire bourgeois society. In these crises a large part, not only of the existing products, but also of the previously created forces of production are destroyed at regular intervals. In these crises, a social epidemic breaks out that, in all earlier epochs, would have seemed an absurdity – the epidemic of overproduction. Society finds itself suddenly pulled back to a condition of momentary barbarism. A famine or a shattering war of universal proportions seems to have severed all means of subsistence. Industry and commerce seem to be annihilated. And why? Because society possesses too much civilization, too many of the necessaries of life, too much industry, and too much commerce. The forces of production at society's

disposal no longer serve as an instrument for the development of bourgeois civilization and its conditions of property. On the contrary, they have become too powerful for these conditions that confine them, and as soon as they surpass this hindrance, they bring the whole of bourgeois society into disorder and jeopardize the existence of bourgeois property. Bourgeois societal conditions have become too narrow to incorporate the wealth created by them. And how does the bourgeoisie withstand these crises? On the one hand, by the enforced obliteration of a mass of forces of production; on the other, by the conquest of new markets and the more methodical exploitation of the old ones. Then, by what means? By paving the way for more universal and dangerous crises, and by reducing the means of preventing them.

(34) The weapons with which the bourgeoisie overcame feudalism are now redirected against the bourgeoisie itself.

(35) But the bourgeoisie has not only built the weapons that bring its own destruction – it has also conjured up the people who are to wield these weapons: they are the modern workers, the proletarians.

(36) In proportion as the bourgeoisie – that is, capital – develops, so also does the proletariat, the modern working class, a class of labourers who live only as long as they have a job, and who have a job only as long as their labour increases capital. These workers, who must sell themselves by piecemeal, are a commodity like all other merchandise and, therefore, are equally subjected to all the

vicissitudes of the competition and to all fluctuations of the market.

(37) Through the division of labour and the increase in the number of machineries, the work of the proletarians has lost all its individual character, and therefore all its appeal to the workers. They become mere accessories to the machines, since only the simplest, most repetitive, and most disengaging skills are required of them. The expense that a worker causes is hence restricted almost entirely to the means of subsistence needed for his maintenance and for the propagation of his species. The price of a commodity, and consequently also of labour, equals its production cost. Thus, in proportion as the work becomes more unpleasant, wages decrease. Moreover, in proportion as there is an increase in machinery use and labour division, there is also an increase in the amount of labour, whether by addition of extra working hours, augmentation of the work to be performed at a certain time, boosted-up speed of the machines, and so on.

(38) Modern industry has transformed the little workshop of the patriarchal master into the great factory of the industrial capitalist. Large masses of workers, all crowded in the factory, are organized like soldiers. As industrial privates, they are placed under the command of a complete hierarchy of officers and sergeants. They are not only the slaves of the bourgeois class and state, but also prisoners of the machine and of the supervisor, and above all, of the individual bourgeois manufacturer himself. This despotism is the more despicable, loathsome, and poisoning since gain is overtly proclaimed to be its only end.

(39) In proportion as manual labour implies less physical effort and skill, that is, the more modern industry develops, the more is the labour of men replaced by that of women and children. Differences in sex and age no longer exercise any validity for the working class. Workers now are nothing else but some instruments of labour with different costs, according to their age and sex.

(40) When the exploitation of the workers by the manufacturer is so far at an end that they receive their salaries in cash, then they are set upon by the other segments of the bourgeoisie – the landlord, the shopkeeper, the pawnbroker, etc.

(41) The petty middle class existing up to now – the small industrialists, tradesmen and rentiers, the craftspeople and the farmers – all these classes gradually sink down into the proletariat, partly because their small capital is insufficient to carry on large-scale industry and is finally defeated in the competition with the large capitalists, partly because their skills are rendered worthless by the newly implemented methods of production. Hence, the proletariat is recruited from all classes of the populace.

(42) The proletariat passes through various stages of development, its struggle beginning at the very hour of its birth.

(43) At its advent, the struggle is carried on by individual workers; afterwards, by the workers of a factory, and then by the workers of a trade in a certain locality versus the individual bourgeois who directly exploits them. They direct their attacks not only against the bourgeois system of production, but also against the instruments of

production themselves. They destroy imported commodities that compete with their own, they smash to pieces machineries, they set factories on fire, and eventually seek to regain by force the estranged status of the medieval worker.

(44) At this stage, the workers form a disorganized mass, which is spread out throughout the country, and is divided by competition. A more compact union is not the result of their own amalgamation, but rather the consequence of the unification of the bourgeoisie, which, in order to attain its own political goals, is forced to set the whole proletariat in motion, and, for the time being, is still able to do so. That is why, at this stage, the proletarians do not fight their own foes, but the foes of their foes – the relics of absolute monarchy, the landowners, the non-industrial bourgeois, and the petty bourgeoisie. The entire course of historical evolution is thus, as yet, concentrated in the hands of the bourgeoisie: indeed, each victory that is obtained is a victory won for the bourgeoisie.

(45) However, with the development of the industry, the proletariat not only increases in number, but it also becomes condensed into larger masses. At the same time, its might intensifies, and the proletariat becomes conscious of its own power. The interests and life standards of the proletariat are increasingly stabilized, as machineries more and more wipe out divisions of labour, and almost everywhere decrease salaries to the same low levels. The growing competition among the bourgeois and the commercial crises that result from it cause the workers' wages to be constantly more variable, while the incessant improvement of machineries, which are now developing

faster than ever, makes their conditions of life even more unsteady; clashes between individual workers and individual bourgeois take more and more the character of clashes between classes. Consequently, the workers begin to form groups that rise against the bourgeois, getting together in order to maintain their salaries. They even set up permanent associations in order to provision themselves for these occasional revolts. Here and there, the struggle may even take the form of riots.

(46) From time to time, the workers are triumphant, but not for long. The outcome of their struggle is not an immediate advantage, but rather the ever-growing unification of the workers. This amalgamation is favoured by the improving means of communication that are created by large-scale industry, whereby the workers belonging to the most distant areas are placed in contact with one another. It was simply this contact that was needed to centralize the many local struggles, which had all the same characteristics, into a national struggle among classes. Nevertheless, each class struggle is a political struggle. And that unification, which took centuries for the burghers of the Middle Ages, with their pitiful roads, to attain is now accomplished in only a few years by the modern proletarians, thanks to railways.

(47) This organization of the proletarians into a class, and therewith into a political party, is at every point shattered again by the competition among the workers themselves. Nonetheless, it always rises up again, stronger, more unwavering, and more resolute than ever. It compels the recognition of the workers' legislative interests by

making use of the divisions within the bourgeoisie itself – for instance, the creation of Ten Hours Bill in England.

(48) Collisions among the classes of the old society, on the whole, are favourable to the development of the proletariat in many ways. The bourgeoisie finds itself involved in a continuous struggle: first, against the aristocracy; later on, against that part of itself whose interests have become opposed to the development of the industry; and always against the bourgeoisie of every foreign country. In all these struggles, the bourgeoisie finds itself obligated to appeal to the proletariat, to ask for its assistance, and thus to draw it into the political arena. So, the bourgeoisie itself supplies the proletariat with its own educational elements, such as weapons for fighting against itself.

(49) Furthermore, as we have already seen, huge portions of the ruling class are, through the development of industry, thrown into the ranks of the proletariat, or at least are threatened in their conditions of existence. These also provide the proletariat new elements of progress.

(50) Finally, in times when the pronouncement of the class struggle draws near, the process of dissolution within the ruling class and, in fact, within the whole of the old society, assumes such a powerful and conspicuous role that a small part of the ruling class breaks free from it and joins the revolutionary class, the only one that holds the future in its hands. Therefore, just as previously a segment of the nobility went over to the bourgeoisie, so now a section of the bourgeoisie joins the proletariat and, particularly, a portion of the bourgeois ideologists who

have elevated themselves to the platform of theoretically understanding the course of historical evolution in its entirety.

(51) Of all classes that face up to the bourgeoisie these days, only the proletariat is a truly revolutionary class. The other classes decay and finally fade away when confronted with large-scale industry. Indeed, the proletariat is its most representative product.

(52) The intermediate class – the small manufacturer, the shopkeeper, the artisan, the farmer – all these fight against the bourgeoisie in order to save from perishing their very existence as middle strata. For that reason, they are not revolutionaries, but conservatives. More than that – they are reactionaries, for they attempt to turn back the wheel of history. And when they happen to be revolutionary, they are so in view of their imminent absorption into the proletariat. In this way, they defend not their present, but their future interests, thus abandoning their own point of view in order to take up that of the proletariat.

(53) The rags proletarians, this slowly decomposing underlayer of the old social system, are swept into the movement by a proletarian revolution. The life standard of this population generally makes it, however, an easily available instrument of corruption for the purpose of reactionary schemes.

(54) The conditions of the old society are already cancelled in those of the proletariat. The proletarian has no property; the relation to his wife and children has no longer anything in common with the bourgeois family

relationship; modern industrial labour and subjection to capital – the same in England as in France, and in America as in Germany – have robbed him of his national character. Laws, morality, and religion are to him nothing else but bourgeois prejudices, which conceal so many bourgeois interests.

(55) All the previous foremost classes sought to preserve the status they had already acquired by imposing the conditions under which they appropriated it. The proletarians can gain possession of the productive forces of society only by abolishing their earlier mode of appropriation, and thereby every other previous mode of appropriation. The proletarians have nothing of their own to secure; their task is to destroy all formerly existing private securities and guarantees of individual possessions.

(56) All previous historical movements were movements of minorities or in the interest of minorities. The proletarian movement is the independent movement of the great majority, in the interest of the great majority. The proletariat, which is the lowest stratum of society at this time, cannot raise itself up, cannot stir itself erect without disrupting and dislocating entirely the overlayers that make up official society.

(57) In form, though not in substance, the struggle of the proletariat with the bourgeoisie is firstly a national one. The proletariat of every country must, certainly, first settle accounts with its own bourgeoisie.

(58) In illustrating the most general phases of the development of the proletariat, we followed the tracks of the more or less disguised civil war pervading existing

society to the point where it bursts out into an open revolution, and where the armed overthrow of the bourgeoisie establishes the basis for the rule of the proletariat.

(59) We have already seen that all previous forms of society have been based on the antagonism of oppressing and oppressed classes. But in order to be able to oppress a class, certain conditions must be secured for at least continuing its servile existence. In the time of serfdom, the serf bettered his status by becoming a member of the commune, and in a similar way the petty bourgeois could become an upper-scale bourgeois under the yoke of feudal absolutism. The modern worker, on the contrary, instead of improving his condition with the progress of industry, sinks deeper and deeper below the life standard of his own class. He turns into a pauper, and pauperism develops more rapidly than population and wealth. From this, it appears that the bourgeoisie is incapable of remaining the ruling class in society any longer, at the same time being incapable of imposing the conditions of existence of its own class upon society in the form of domineering legislations. The bourgeoisie is unable to rule because it is not capable to assure the bare conditions of existence for its slaves, even within the limits of their slavery, and this is because it has to let them sink into such a position that it has to feed them instead of being fed by them. Society can no longer live under this class – that is, its existence is no longer compatible with that of society.

(60) The most indispensable condition for the existence of the bourgeois class and for its dominance is the accumulation of wealth in the hands of private individuals

through the formation and increase of capital. The condition upon which capital is amassed is wage-labour. The wage-labour system is based exclusively on competition among workers. The advance of industry – whose indirect and overpowering supporter is the bourgeoisie – replaces the isolation of the workers – which occurs because of competition – with the workers' revolutionary alliance, which is due to association. Therefore, with the advent of large-scale industry, the very ground upon which the bourgeoisie manufactures and appropriates products is pulled from under its feet. Above all, the result of what the bourgeoisie produces is its own undertakers. That is why, the downfall of the bourgeoisie and the rise of the proletariat are both inevitable.

II

Proletarians and Communists

(61) Generally, what kind of relation exists between the communists and the proletarians?

(62) The communists form no separate party in opposition to the other workers' parties.

(63) They have no interest different from that of the proletariat as a whole.

(64) They lay down no particular principles of their own on which they wish to shape and pattern the proletariat movement.

(65) The communists are distinguished from the other proletariat parties only by the fact that, on the one hand, in the different national struggles of the proletarians, they point out and stress the importance of the common interests of the proletariat as a whole, independently of all nationality; and that, on the other hand, in the various phases of development which the struggle of the proletariat against the bourgeoisie passes through, they always represent the interests of the entire movement.

(66) Practically, the communists are the most progressive and unwavering section of every country's working class parties, always pressing forward. As for theory, they have an advantage over the great bulk of the proletariat: the communists clearly understand the conditions, the march line, and the general results of the proletariat movement.

(67) The communists' immediate aim is identical with that of the other proletarian parties – organization of the proletariat as a class, abolishment of bourgeois supremacy, and conquest of political power by the proletariat.

(68) The theoretical precepts of the communists are not based on ideas or principles that have been invented or discovered by this or that so-called universal reformer.

(69) Their precepts are merely general expressions of the actual relations in an existing class struggle, the conditions of a historical movement unfolding before our

very eyes. The abolition of existing property relations does not constitute a distinctive characteristic of communism.

(70) All property relations have been subject to a continuous historical changeover, to a perpetual historical transformation.

(71) The French Revolution, for instance, abolished feudal property in favour of bourgeois property.

(72) Therefore, it is not the abolition of property in general that which distinguishes communism, but rather the abolition of bourgeois property.

(73) But modern bourgeois private property is the ultimate, most complex expression of the system's creation and appropriation of products that is based on class antagonisms, and on the exploitation of humans by humans.

(74) In this way, the communists can sum up their theory in one single phrase – abolition of private property.

(75) Communists have been accused of wanting to abolish property that has been acquired through hard work, that is, property which is said to be the basis of all personal freedom, activity, and independence.

(76) Hard-gained, self-acquired, self-earned property! Are you talking about the property of the petty bourgeois and the small farmer, which precedes the present system of bourgeois property? We do not need to abolish that: the progress of industry has already abolished it, and is abolishing it on a daily basis.

(77) Or are you talking about modern bourgeois private property?

(78) But does labour under the wage system – that is, the proletarians' labour – create any property for them? Not at all. It creates capital, in other words property which exploits wage labour, and which can only increase on condition of giving birth to a new supply of wage labour, just to exploit it anew. Property, in its present-day form, is centred around the antagonism of capital and wage labour. Let us examine both sides of this antagonism. To be a capitalist means to occupy not only a personal, but also a social position in the production system.

(79) Capital is a collective product and can be activated only by the joint exertions of many members or, in the last resort, only by the united efforts of all members of society.

(80) That is why capital is not a personal power, but a social one.

(81) Therefore, when capital is transformed into collective property that belongs to all members of society, personal property is not thereby converted into social property. Only the social character of property is changed. In this way, property loses its class character.

(82) Let us now turn to wage labour.

(83) The average price of wage labour is the minimum wage – that is the quantity of means of subsistence necessary to maintain the existence of the worker for the purpose of working. What the wage worker gains by means of his work is hardly sufficient for the bare reproduction of his existence. We by no means wish to abolish this personal appropriation of the products of labour for the purpose of reproducing human life – a gain which

leaves no net surplus that can confer power in order to command the labour of others. We wish only to abolish the miserably insufficient character of this appropriation, under which the worker lives only to increase capital and is permitted to live only insofar as the interests of the ruling class require it.

(84) In bourgeois society, living labour is nothing else but a means of increasing accumulated labour. In communist society, accumulated labour is only a means of widening, increasing, and fostering the worker's life standard.

(85) Therefore, in bourgeois society the past rules over the present, while in communist society the present reigns over the past. In bourgeois society, capital is independent and personalized, while the active individual is dependent and depersonalized.

(86) And the abolition of this state of such a system is called by the bourgeois abolition of independence and personality. And rightly so, for the question in hand is the abolishment of bourgeois personality, independence, and freedom.

(87) By freedom, under the present bourgeois conditions of production, is understood free trade, and freedom of purchasing and selling.

(88) But if trade, altogether, falls, so will free trade fall with the rest. The declamations about free trade, like all the rest of our bourgeoisie's raving about freedom in general, have a meaning only in contrast with limited trade, with the enslaved tradesmen of the Middle Ages, but they have no meaning whatsoever when opposed to the

communist abolition of huckstering, of the bourgeois conditions of production, and of the bourgeoisie itself.

(89) You are horrified because we aim at abolishing private property. But in your existing society, private property is abolished for nine-tenths of the population: it exists because for nine-tenths it does not exist at all. You reproach us, therefore, that we intend to abolish a form of property which involves, as a necessary condition, the absence of all property for the great majority of society.

(90) To put it in a nutshell, you tax us with aiming to abolish your property. That is exactly what we want to do.

(91) From the moment labour can no longer be turned into such capital as money, or rent, that means into a monopolizing social power, from the moment individual property can no longer be converted into bourgeois property – from that moment, you say, the role of the individual is abolished.

(92) You acknowledge therefore that by "individual" you mean no other person than the bourgeois, the owner of the bourgeois property. And, truly, the role of this individual must be abolished.

(93) Communism deprives no one of the right of owning the products of society. Communism only takes away the power of owning the command over other people's labour.

(94) It has been objected that, with the abolition of private property, all work will cease, and universal laziness will infuse society.

(95) According to this, bourgeois society ought, long since, to have gone down under through laziness; for those of its members who work do not acquire any property, and those who do acquire property do not work at all. This whole objection amounts to the tautological proposition according to which there can no longer be any wage labour as soon as capital ceases to exist.

(96) All objections raised against the communist mode of production and appropriation of material products have, in a similar way, been directed against the appropriation and production of intellectual goods. Just as, for the bourgeois, the annihilation of class property involves the cessation of appropriation, likewise, the annihilation of class culture, for them, is identical with the disappearance of all culture.

(97) The culture whose loss they lament is, for the great majority, simply an upbringing system according to which humans are turned into machines.

(98) But do not fight with us, while you measure the proposed abolition of bourgeois property according to your bourgeois notions of freedom, culture, justice, etc. Your ideas are themselves products of the outcome of the bourgeois conditions of production and property, just as your justice is only the will of your class turned into a law for all, a will whose subject is set by the economical conditions of existence of your class.

(99) The selfish conception whereby you transform your conditions of production and property from historical relations that emerge and vanish in the production process into eternal laws of reason and nature is the conception that

you share with all ruling classes that have preceded you. What you comprehend with regard to ancient and feudal property, this you are forbidden to comprehend with regard to bourgeois property.

(100) Abolition of the family! Even the most radical are shaken by this outrageous intention of the communists.

(101) What does the present-day family, the bourgeois family, rest on? It rests on capital, on private gain. In a completely developed form, it only exists for the bourgeoisie. However, it finds its complement in the enforced celibacy of the proletariat and in public prostitution.

(102) The bourgeois family will naturally disappear when its complement ceases to exist, and both will vanish with the disappearance of capital.

(103) Do you reproach us that we want to abolish the exploitation of children by their parents? We plead guilty to this crime. But, you say, we destroy the most endearing relationships by replacing home education with social education.

(104) And is not your education also determined by society, by the social conditions under which you educate, by the direct or indirect involvement of society through schools, etc.? The communists have not fabricated the impact of society on education; they only change its character in order to rescue education from the influence of a ruling class.

(105) The bourgeois talk about family, education, and the intimate connection between parents and children,

become all the more abhorring, the more, by the action of large-scale industry, all family ties for proletarians are destroyed, and the children are changed into mere commercial articles and instruments of labour.

(106) "But you, communists, intend to introduce the community of women," the entire bourgeoisie screams at us in chorus.

(107) The bourgeois man looks upon his wife as a simple instrument of production. He hears that instruments of production are to be exploited in common, and naturally he can only conclude that women's destiny is to be used up in common.

(108) The bourgeois man does not suspect that the goal aimed at is to abolish the very status of women as mere instruments of production.

(109) For the rest, nothing is more ridiculous than the extreme moral revulsion displayed by our bourgeois at the community of women which, they claim, is officially founded by the communists. The communists have no need to introduce community of women – it has almost always existed.

(110) Our bourgeois, unhappy with having only the wives and daughters of the proletarians at their disposal, not to mention the official prostitutes, enjoy immensely seducing one another's wives.

(111) Bourgeois marriage is in reality a community of wives. At the most, then, communists can only be reproached with wishing to replace a transparent and legal community of women with a hypocritically opaque one.

Moreover, it is evident that with the abolition of the present conditions of production there also vanishes the community of women springing from these conditions – and that is both official and unofficial prostitution.

(112) The communists are further reproached with intending to destroy the idea of fatherland and the spirit of nationality.

(113) The workers have no fatherland. You cannot take from people something they do not have. In that the proletariat must first obtain political supremacy, rise to the status of national class, and constitute itself as the nation, it is itself still national, even though not in the bourgeois sense of the term.

(114) National divisions and antagonisms among peoples are already vanishing more and more through the development of the bourgeoisie, with freedom of commerce, the world market, uniformity in the mode of production, and the subsequent life standards.

(115) The rule of the proletariat will cause them to disappear even faster. United action, at least on the part of the civilized countries, is one of the imperatives of proletarian emancipation.

(116) In proportion as the exploitation of one individual by another is abolished, the exploitation of one country by another will also be abolished.

(117) The hostile attitudes of the nations to one another will stop with the antagonisms of the classes into which each nation is divided.

(118) The charges against communism made from religious, philosophical, and, generally, ideological standpoints do not deserve a real discussion.

(119) Does it require any great degree of intellect to understand that people's ideas, points of view, and conceptions – in a word, their consciousness – change along with their material conditions, social relations, and social life?

(120) What else does the history of ideas show than that intellectual production has always changed along with the transformations in material production? The ruling ideas of every age have always been the ideas of the ruling class.

(121) People talk about ideas that have revolutionized society. However, they merely express the fact that within the old form of society, the elements of a new one have been configured, and that the dissolution of the old ideas keeps pace with the dissolution of the old conditions of life.

(122) When the ancient world was at its apogee, Christianity triumphed over the old religions. When Christian ideas succumbed, in the 18th century, to the ideas of the Enlightenment, feudal society was fighting its last death battle with the then revolutionary bourgeoisie. The ideas of freedom of conscience and freedom of religion were the expressions of free competition in the sphere of conscience.

(123) "But," it will be said, "religious, moral, philosophical, political, juridical ideas, and so on have certainly been changed in the course of historical

development. Religion, morality, philosophy, politics, and law always survived these alterations.

(124) Moreover, there are eternal truths such as freedom, justice, etc. that are common to all societal phases. Communism, nevertheless, abolishes eternal truths, and it also abolishes religion and morality, instead of just remoulding them anew; it therefore contradicts all the past modes of historical progress."

(125) What does this accusation amount to? The history of all preceding society has developed in class antagonisms that assumed different forms in different epochs.

(126) Whatever form these antagonisms may have taken, the exploitation of one part of society by the other is a fact common to all past centuries. No wonder, then, that the social consciousness of the past, in its entirety, should have a common ground, despite all the multiplicity and diversity it displays: that it should move in certain common forms of consciousness which will completely vanish only with the total disappearance of class antagonism.

(127) The communist revolution is the most radical rupture with the traditional property relations: no wonder, then, that its development will involve the most radical break with traditional ideas.

(128) However, let us get through with the bourgeois accusations against communism.

(129) We have seen above that the first step in the workers' revolution is the elevation of the proletariat to the

position of ruling class, which is the conquest of democracy.

(130) The proletariat will make use of its political supremacy to gradually deprive the bourgeoisie of the control of capital, centralize all instruments of production in the hands of the state – that is, the proletariat organized as the ruling class – , and augment the total of productive forces as quickly as possible.

(131) In the beginning, of course, this can only be achieved through despotic interference with the right of property and the bourgeois conditions of production – hence, by measures which appear economically inadequate and untenable, but which, in the course of the action surpass their own limits, and are unavoidable as a means of entirely changing the modes of production.

(132) Certainly, every country will have a different set of measures.

(133) Nonetheless, for the most advanced countries the following will be fairly generally applicable:

1. Abolition of land property and application of land rent to the public revenue.
2. Heavy progressive taxation.
3. Abolition of the right of inheritance.
4. Confiscation of the property of all émigrés and rebels.
5. Centralization of credit in the hands of the state through a national bank with state capital and an exclusive monopoly.
6. Centralization of the entire transportation network in the hands of the state.

7. Increase in the number of national factories and instruments of production; the cultivation of wastelands and improvement of land according to a common plan.
8. Equal obligation to work for all; the creation of industrial armies, especially for agriculture.
9. The union of manufacturing and agricultural industries in order to gradually eliminate the distinction between city and countryside.
10. Free education for all children in public schools; abolition of factory labour for children in its present form; combination of education and material production, etc.

(134) When, in the process of development, class distinctions have finally disappeared and all production is concentrated in the hands of associated people, the public power loses its political character. Political power, in the exact sense of the word, is the organized power of one class for the oppression of another. If the proletariat, during its struggle against the bourgeoisie, is forced under the circumstances to become a class, makes itself a class through a revolution, and, as such, abolishes by force the old conditions of production, then along with the relations of production it also destroys the conditions for the existence of class antagonism and of classes in general, and thereby its own rule as a class.

(135) In place of the old bourgeois society, with its classes and class antagonisms, we will have an association wherein the free development of each is the precondition for the free development of all.

III

Socialist and Communist Literature

1. Reactionary Socialism

(a) Feudal Socialism

(136) In accordance with their historical positions, the French and English aristocracies developed a vocation for writing pamphlets against modern bourgeois society. In the French July Revolution of 1830 and in the English reform movement, they once again succumbed to the much-loathed upstart. There could be no longer any question about a serious political struggle. A literary struggle alone remained for them. But even in the sphere of literature the old rhetoric of the Restoration had become impossible. In order to arouse sympathy, the aristocracy had to apparently lose sight of its own interests and formulate its accusation against the bourgeoisie in the interest of the exploited working class. In this way, the aristocrats took revenge on their new rulers by singing lampoons and murmuring frightening prophecies of coming woe.

(137) In this way sprang out feudal socialism – half lamentation, half libel song; half echo of the past, half menace of the future, at times striking the very heart of the bourgeoisie's heart by its bitter and sarcastic comments,

always comic in its effect through its total incapacity to understand the course of modern history.

(138) They waved the proletarian alms-bag as a banner, in order to rally the people around them. But whenever the people joined them, they saw on their hindquarters the old feudal coats of arms, and scattered away with loud and mocking laughter.

(139) A section of the French Legitimists and the party of Young England played their roles in this pageant.

(140) When the feudalists point out that their mode of exploitation was different from that of the bourgeoisie, they forget that they exploited under totally different and now obsolete circumstances and conditions. When they show that under their rule the modern proletariat never existed, they forget that the modern bourgeoisie is the necessary offspring of their own social order.

(141) For the rest, they hide the reactionary nature of their criticism so little that their main accusation against the bourgeoisie is that of having created a class which is meant to sever the whole of the old social order.

(142) Hence, the reason for blaming the bourgeoisie is not so much the fact that it has created a revolutionary proletariat, but rather the fact that the bourgeoisie has created a proletariat at all.

(143) Therefore, in their political practice they take part in all coercive measures against the working class, and in everyday life, despite all their puffed-up rhetoric, they stoop to pick up the golden apples and to barter loyalty,

love, and honour for the traffic in wool, sugar beets, and schnapps.

(144) Even as the priest has always gone hand in hand with the feudal landlord, so has clerical socialism with feudal socialism.

(145) Nothing is easier than to give Christian asceticism a socialist veneer. Has not Christianity condemned private property, marriage, and the state? Has it not preached charity and mendicancy, celibacy and mortification of the flesh, monastic life and the Church in the place of these things? Religious socialism is the holy water with which the priest blesses the vexation of the aristocrat.

(b) Petty-Bourgeois Socialism

(146) The feudal aristocracy is not the only class that was destroyed by the bourgeoisie, and whose conditions of existence became exhausted and died out in modern bourgeois society. The medieval burgess and the small farm owner were the precursors of the modern bourgeoisie. In countries with a small degree of industrial and commercial development, this class still vegetates alongside the rising bourgeoisie.

(147) In countries where modern civilization has developed, a new class of petty bourgeois has been formed. This class ebbs and flows between the proletariat and the bourgeoisie, and continually regenerates itself as a supplementary part of bourgeois society. The members of

this class are constantly hurled down into the proletariat by competition, and, truly, with the development of the large-scale industrial system they even see a time approaching when they will entirely disappear as an independent segment of modern society, only to be replaced in manufacturing, commerce, and agriculture by supervisors and superintendents.

(148) In countries like France, where far more than one half of the population are peasants, it was natural that writers who sided with the proletariat against the bourgeoisie should apply the standards of the small peasantry and the petty bourgeoisie in their critique of the bourgeois regime and take the side of the workers from the standpoint of the petty bourgeoisie. In this way arose petty-bourgeois socialism. Sismondi [Swiss historian and economist] is the leading figure in this literature, not only in France, but also in England.

(149) This form of socialism dissected with great acuteness the contradictions in the modern conditions of production, and laid bare the hypocritical apologetics of the economists. It indubitably proved the disastrous effects of machinery and the division of labour, the concentration of capital and land property in only a few hands, overproduction, crises, the needed ruin of the small bourgeois and peasants, the misery of the proletariat, anarchy in production, the scandalous inequalities in the distribution of wealth, the industrial fight to the knife among nations, and the dissolution of traditional moral rules, family relationships, and nationalities.

(150) Nevertheless, in terms of its positive aims, this type of socialism aspires either to re-establish the old means of production and exchange, and along with them the old property conditions and the old society in its entirety, or to confine by force the modern means of production and exchange within the framework of the old property conditions which they blast, and had to blast by all means. In both cases, this Socialism is, at the same time, reactionary and utopian.

(151) The corporate guilds in manufactures, and a patriarchal agriculture – these are its last words.

(152) In its further development, this form of socialism exhausted itself in foolish lamentations over a glass of inebriating liquor.

(c) German or True Socialism

(153) The Socialist and Communist literature of France – which originated under the impress of the bourgeois regime in power, and which is the literary expression of the struggle against this rule – was introduced into Germany at a time when the bourgeoisie had just begun its battle against feudal absolutism.

(154) German philosophers, half-philosophers, and every intellectual *bel esprit* eagerly seized on this literature and forgot that when these writings emigrated from France, the French conditions of life did not travel to Germany along with them. Connected with German conditions, this French literature lost all immediate practical significance

and assumed a merely literary facet. It could only appear as an idle speculation about the best form of society and the realization of the true nature of human beings. In a similar fashion, for the German philosophers of the 18th century, the demands of the first French Revolution were noting more than the requirements imposed by "practical reason" in general, and the expression of the will of the revolutionary French bourgeoisie was, in their vision, the law of the pure will, of will as it ought to be, of truly human will.

(155) The only noteworthy job done by the German litterateurs consisted in bringing the new French ideas into accordance with their old philosophic conscience, or, rather, in appropriating the French ideas without abandoning their own philosophic points of view.

(156) This appropriation was carried out in the same way one masters a foreign language, namely by translation.

(157) It is well known how the monks wrote insipid hagiographies based on the manuscripts recording the classical works of the ancient heathen world. The German men of letters did the very opposite with the profane French literature. They wrote their philosophical nonsense beneath the French original. For instance, beneath the French criticism of the monetary system, they wrote "estrangement of human nature"; beneath the French criticism of the bourgeois state, they wrote "abolition of the pre-eminence of the abstract universals," and so forth.

(158) They labelled the foisting of their philosophic phraseology underneath the French investigations with such names as "philosophy of action," "true socialism,"

“German science of socialism,” “philosophical foundation of socialism, etc.

(159) The socialist-communist literature of France was thus entirely emasculated. And when it ceased, in German hands, to express the struggle of one class against another, the onesidedness of representing the requirements of truthfulness rather than true requirements, and of the interests of human nature, that is, of humanity generally, which belongs to no class, it was found to have no real foundation, since it existed in the hazy realms of philosophic fantasy alone.

(160) This German socialism, which did its gauche assignments with so much gravity and solemnity, and then cried them up along the street even as market paddler, gradually lost its pedantic innocence.

(161) The struggle of the German, and especially of the Prusssian bourgeoisie, against feudalism and absolute monarchy, in short, the liberal movement, became more serious.

(162) True socialism was in this way offered its long wished-for opportunity of placing socialist demands in opposition to the actual course of politics, of hurling the traditional anathemas against liberalism, the constitutional government, bourgeois competition, bourgeois freedom of the press, bourgeois legislation, bourgeois notions of liberty and equality, and of preaching to the masses of people that they had nothing to gain, and everything to lose, from this bourgeois movement. German socialism forgot, quite fortunately, that the French criticism – whose prosaic echo it was – presupposed modern bourgeois society with the corresponding material conditions of life and the suitable

political constitution – the very presumptions whose fulfillment only at this time became a real issue in Germany.

(163) To the German absolute governments and their followers – priests, schoolmasters, cabbage-junkers, and bureaucrats – socialism served as a welcome scarecrow against the threat of the rising bourgeoisie.

(164) It was a piece of candy given after the floggings and shootings with which these same governments replied to the German working-class insurrections.

(165) While true socialism thus served the governments as a weapon against the German bourgeoisie, it also directly represented a reactionary interest, namely that of the German petty-bourgeois philistines. In Germany, the petty bourgeoisie – a class remaining since the 16th century, and since then always renewing itself under slightly different guises – constitutes the actual social basis of the existing state of things.

(166) The preservation of this class is the preservation of the existing order of things in Germany. From the industrial and political supremacy of the bourgeoisie, it fears annihilation, on the one hand, as a consequence of the concentration of capital, and on the other hand, the creation of a revolutionary proletariat. In its eyes, true Socialism seemed to kill two birds with one stone. It spread like an epidemic.

(167) The robe of speculative cobwebs, embroidered with flowers of speech, steeped in the dew of nauseating sugary sentimentality – this super gushing robe in which the German socialists wrapped the remains of

their “eternal” truths only increased the sale of their commodity to this public.

(168) On its part, German socialism recognized more and more its calling as the grandiloquent representative of the petty-bourgeois philistines.

(169) It proclaimed the German nation to be the emblematic nation and the German philistine to be the archetypal human being. To each cruel meanness of this “archetypal” human being, it gave a hidden, higher, socialistic interpretation in which it meant exactly the opposite. It eventually reached the limit by directly opposing the destructive tendency of communism, and by proclaiming its own impartial sovereignty over all class struggles. With very few exceptions, all the so-called socialist and communist writings circulating in Germany belong to the area of this tainted and annoying type of literature.

2. Conservative or Bourgeois Socialism

(170) A part of the bourgeoisie wishes to alleviate social ills, in order to secure the existence of bourgeois society.

(171) To this section belong economists, philanthropists, humanitarians, improvers of the condition of the working class, charity fundraisers, opponents to cruelty to animals, temperance advocates, and hole-and-corner reformers of the most varied kinds. And this bourgeois socialism has, moreover, been worked out into compact systems.

(172) As an example, we cite Proudhon's [French early anarchist] *Philosophy of Poverty* [a text, criticized by Marx, that analyzes the contradictions between fact and right in social economy].

(173) The socialist bourgeois want the life standard of modern society without the accompanying struggles and dangers. They want the existing state of society, minus the revolutionary and destructive elements it contains. The bourgeoisie conceives the world in which it rules as naturally the best possible world. Bourgeois socialism takes this comforting conception up to a partial or a complete system. When it requires the proletariat to put its system into effect in order to march straightforward into New Jerusalem, it asks in reality that the proletariat should socially remain within the limits of the present day, and at the same time cast off its hateful ideas concerning that society.

(174) A second, less systematic and more practical form of socialism attempted at depreciating every revolutionary movement in the eyes of the working class by showing that their condition cannot improve by an ordinary change, but only by a transformation of their material and economic conditions of existence. However, through a transformation of the material conditions of existence, these socialists do not mean the abolition of the bourgeois relations of production, which can be implemented only by a revolution, but rather administrative reforms, to be operated within the limits of the old system, which, consequently, will not change anything in the relations between capital and wage-labour, but at most will just

simplify the details and decrease the cost of bourgeois government.

(175) Bourgeois Socialism attains its most fitting expression only when it becomes simply a figure of speech.

(176) Free trade! – for the benefit of the working class. Protective tariffs! – for the benefit of the working class. Individual prison cells! – for the benefit of the working class. This is the last word of bourgeois socialism, the only earnest word.

(177) Its socialism consists in declaring that the bourgeois are bourgeois for the benefit of the working class.

3. Critical-Utopian Socialism and Communism

(178) We do not speak here of the literature that in all the great revolutions of modern times has addressed the demands of the proletariat (Babeuf's writings, etc.).

(179) The proletariat's first attempts to pursue its own class interests, made at a time of general excitement during which the feudal society was overthrown, necessarily failed, owing to the then undeveloped state of the proletariat itself, as well as to the lack of material conditions for its emancipation, conditions which were only the product of the bourgeois era. This revolutionary literature that accompanied these first movements of the proletariat had necessarily a reactionary content. It taught a form of universal asceticism and social equality through rough levelling.

(180) The socialist and communist system proper, the systems of St. Simon, Fourier, Owen [the so-called "utopian socialists"] and others emerge in the early, undeveloped period of the struggle between proletariat and bourgeoisie, which we have described above (see "Bourgeoisie and Proletariat").

(181) The creators of these systems see, truly, the class antagonisms, as well as the process of the dissolving elements within the dominant social system. However, they do not perceive any historical self-initiating activity; nor do they observe any characteristic political movement on the part of the proletariat.

(182) Since the development of class antagonism keeps pace with the development of industry, they accordingly could not find the material conditions for the emancipation of the proletariat. Therefore, they began to search for a social science and for social laws in order to create these conditions.

(183) Social activity has to yield to their personal inventive activity; historical conditions of emancipation to invented ones; the progressive organization of the proletariat into a class to a societal organization of their own concept. To them, the approaching phase of world history resolves itself into propaganda for their social plans and into putting them into practice.

(184) In their plans, indeed, they are conscious of primarily advocating the interests of the working class as the most suffering class. The proletariat exists for them only from the perspective of being the most suffering class.

(185) The undeveloped form of the class struggle, as well as their own position in society, cause socialists of

this type to consider themselves far superior to the aforementioned class antagonism. They want to improve the material condition of all members of society, including the most favoured. Hence, their consistent appeal to all social classes, with a preference for the dominant class. Certainly, one need only understand their system in order to acknowledge that it is the best possible plan for the best possible form of society.

(186) That is why they reject all political and especially all revolutionary action: truly, they wish to reach their goal in a peaceful manner, and aim, by the force of example, at preparing the way for the new social gospel by conducting small experiments that naturally fail.

(187) This fantastic portrayal of future society at a time when the proletariat is still in a very undeveloped phase, and has but a fantastic conception of its own position, corresponds to the expression of its instinctive want for a general reconstruction of society.

(188) However, the socialist and communist writings contain critical elements as well. They attack each foundation of existing society. Thus, they have offered precious material for the enlightenment of the workers. Their positive measures regarding a future state of society – for example, the abolition of the antagonism between town and country, of the family, of individual profit, of wage-labour, the proclamation of social harmony, the conversion of the state into a mere production supervisor – all these propositions of theirs solely express the abolition of class distinction, which is only just beginning to take shape, and which they still know of only in its early forms, which are

vague and indefinite. Hence, these propositions are still purely utopian in nature.

(189) The significance of critical utopian socialism and communism stands in an inverse relation to historical progress. In proportion as the class struggle develops and assumes a clear form, this imaginary elevation above class struggle and this imaginary resistance to it lose all practical value and theoretical justification. As a consequence, although the creators of these systems were revolutionary in many respects, their disciples invariably form reactionary sects. They hold fast to the traditional views of their masters as against the gradual historical development of the proletariat. They, therefore, consistently strive to dull the class struggle and to reconcile the class antagonism. They still dream of the experimental realization of their social utopias, of establishing isolated phalansteries [buildings designed by Fourier for utopian communities], of founding home colonies, of setting up a little Icaria [utopian community formed in the U.S. by Étienne Cabet, the French philosopher who coined the term "communism" in 1839] – a paperback edition of New Jerusalem – and in order to build all these sand castles, they have to appeal to the philanthropy of bourgeois hearts and pockets. Progressively, they sink into the category of the above-mentioned reactionary or into that of conservative Socialists, and are different from them only by more systematic pedantry and by their fanatical superstitious belief in the miraculous effects of their social science.

(190) That is why they vehemently oppose all political action on the part of the workers, action which could only arise from blind disbelief in the new gospel.

(191) The Owenites [followers of utopian socialist Robert Owen] in England and the Fourierists [followers of utopian socialist Charles Fourier] in France came out against the Chartists [working-class supporters of the People's Charter of 1838 in Britain] and the Reformists [supporters of the Reform Act of 1832 in Britain].

IV

Position of the Communists On the Various Opposition Parties

(192) Section II has clearly indicated the relationship between the communists and the already established workers' parties, hence their relationship to the Chartists in England and the Agrarian Reformers in North America.

(193) The communists fight for the accomplishment of their immediate goals and for the interests of the working class; however, in the present-day movement they are also responsible for the future of the movement. In France, the communists align themselves with the social-democrats against the conservative and radical bourgeoisie, without renouncing their right to take a critical stand in regard to phrases and illusions stemming from the revolutionary tradition.

(194) In Switzerland they support the Radicals, without failing to remember that this party consists of incongruous elements, partly of democratic socialists, in

the French acceptance of the term, and partly of radical bourgeois.

(195) Among the Poles, the communists support the party that makes an agrarian revolution the prerequisite for national emancipation, the very same party that started the Cracow Insurrection of 1846.

(196) In Germany, once the bourgeoisie acts in a revolutionary way, the communists fight alongside the bourgeoisie against the absolute monarchy, feudal proprietorship of land, and the petty bourgeoisie.

(197) Nevertheless, they do not cease, even for a single minute, to inculcate in the workers the clearest possible consciousness of the hostile antagonism between bourgeoisie and proletariat, so that the German workers can immediately take the social and political conditions which the bourgeoisie must necessarily bring about along with its supremacy and turn them into so many weapons against the bourgeoisie, and so that, after the overthrow of the reactionary classes in Germany, the fight against the bourgeoisie itself may immediately begin.

(198) The communists turn their attention mainly to Germany, since this country stands on the eve of a bourgeois revolution and since it is carrying out this insurgency under more advanced conditions of European civilization in general, and with a much more developed proletariat than the English one in the 17th century and the French one in the 18th century; the German bourgeois revolution can thus only be the direct prelude to a proletarian revolution.

(199) In short, the communists everywhere support each revolutionary movement against the existing state of affairs, social and political.

(200) In all these movements, they endeavour to emphasize the property question as the foremost question in each, regardless of its degree of development at the time.

(201) Finally, the communists work everywhere for the unification and alliance of the democratic parties of all countries.

(202) The communists display contempt for concealing their views and aims. They openly declare that their goals can be reached only by forcefully overthrowing all social conditions that have so far been in existence. Let the ruling classes tremble at a communist revolution! The proletarians have nothing to lose in it, save their chains. In fact, they have a world to win.

(203) Proletarians of all countries, unite! [also known as "Workers of the world, unite!"]

[Translation begun on March 27, 2007 and completed on September 19, 2007 in Toronto, Ontario]

www.ingramcontent.com/pod-product-compliance
Ingram Content Group UK Ltd.
Pitfield, Milton Keynes, MK11 3LW, UK
UKHW041835200726
13854UKWH00003BA/1153